This French Notebook Belongs To:

_____

Published by: On Target Publishing
Published in the United States of America

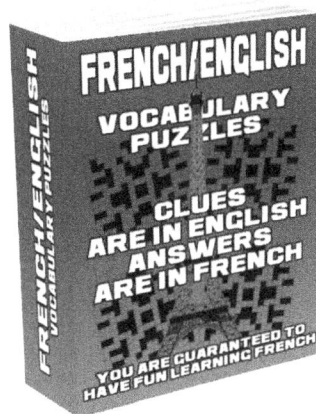

Here is a totally unique concept!

https://www.amazon.com/dp/1080612750

You will Master French and have a lot of fun at the same time! This book has crossword puzzles where the clues are in English and the answers are in French!

Can you work out the words? When you do, you will be learning French without even realizing it!

Then... Move on to the Word Match puzzles.

In these, there is a list of French words and a random ordered list of the English translations. Just match them up! It's easy to do most of them and by looking at the words and definitions that are left over, you'll be surprised how much French you pick up, just by deducing the proper matches!

https://www.amazon.com/dp/1080612750

Get YOUR copy today... You'll like it!

Vocabulary - French	Translation - English

Practice Exercises

Vocabulary - French	Translation - English

Practice Exercises

Vocabulary - French	Translation - English

Practice Exercises

Vocabulary - French	Translation - English

Practice Exercises

Vocabulary - French	Translation - English

Practice Exercises

Vocabulary - French	Translation - English

Practice Exercises

Vocabulary - French	Translation - English

Practice Exercises

Vocabulary - French	Translation - English

Practice Exercises

Vocabulary - French	Translation - English

Practice Exercises

Vocabulary - French	Translation - English

Practice Exercises

Vocabulary - French	Translation - English

Practice Exercises

Vocabulary - French	Translation - English

Practice Exercises

Vocabulary - French	Translation - English

Practice Exercises

Vocabulary - French	Translation - English

Practice Exercises

Vocabulary - French	Translation - English

Practice Exercises

Vocabulary - French	Translation - English

Practice Exercises

Vocabulary - French	Translation - English

Practice Exercises

Vocabulary - French	Translation - English

Practice Exercises

Vocabulary - French	Translation - English

Practice Exercises

Vocabulary - French	Translation - English

Practice Exercises

Vocabulary - French	Translation - English

Practice Exercises

Vocabulary - French	Translation - English

Practice Exercises

Vocabulary - French	Translation - English

Practice Exercises

Vocabulary - French	Translation - English

Practice Exercises

Vocabulary - French	Translation - English

Practice Exercises

Vocabulary - French	Translation - English

Practice Exercises

Vocabulary - French	Translation - English

Practice Exercises

Vocabulary - French	Translation - English

Practice Exercises

Vocabulary - French	Translation - English

Practice Exercises

Vocabulary - French	Translation - English

Practice Exercises

Vocabulary - French	Translation - English

Practice Exercises

Vocabulary - French	Translation - English

Practice Exercises

Vocabulary - French	Translation - English

Practice Exercises

Vocabulary - French	Translation - English

Practice Exercises

Vocabulary - French	Translation - English

Practice Exercises

Vocabulary - French	Translation - English

Practice Exercises

Vocabulary - French	Translation - English

Practice Exercises

Vocabulary - French	Translation - English

Practice Exercises

Vocabulary - French	Translation - English

Practice Exercises

Vocabulary - French	Translation - English

Practice Exercises

Vocabulary - French	Translation - English

Practice Exercises

Vocabulary - French	Translation - English

Practice Exercises

Vocabulary - French	Translation - English

Practice Exercises

Vocabulary - French	Translation - English

Practice Exercises

Vocabulary - French	Translation - English

Practice Exercises

Vocabulary - French	Translation - English

Practice Exercises

Vocabulary - French	Translation - English

Practice Exercises

Vocabulary - French	Translation - English

Practice Exercises

Vocabulary - French	Translation - English

Practice Exercises

Vocabulary - French	Translation - English

Practice Exercises

Vocabulary - French	Translation - English

Practice Exercises

Vocabulary - French	Translation - English

Practice Exercises

Vocabulary - French	Translation - English

Practice Exercises

Vocabulary - French	Translation - English

Practice Exercises

Vocabulary - French	Translation - English

Practice Exercises

Vocabulary - French	Translation - English

Practice Exercises

Vocabulary - French	Translation - English

Practice Exercises

Vocabulary - French	Translation - English

Practice Exercises

Vocabulary - French	Translation - English

Practice Exercises

Vocabulary - French	Translation - English

Practice Exercises

Made in the USA
Las Vegas, NV
07 April 2021